LIZ EARLE'S
QUICK GUIDES

Food
Allergies

LIZ EARLE'S
QUICK GUIDES

Food
Allergies

BOXTREE

Advice to the Reader

Before following any dietary advice contained in this book, it is recommended that you consult your doctor if you suffer from any health problems or special condition or are in any doubt.

First published in Great Britain in 1995 by Boxtree Limited, Broadwall House, 21 Broadwall, London SE1 9PL

10 9 8 7 6 5 4 3 2

ISBN: 0 7522 1675 9

Text design by Blackjacks
Cover design by Hammond Hammond

Printed and Bound in Great Britain by Cox & Wyman Ltd., Reading, Berkshire

A CIP catalogue entry for this book is available from the British Library

Contents

ACKNOWLEDGEMENTS

I am grateful to Midi Fairgreave for helping to produce this book – also to Jenny Rucker, research dietitian at the Department of Gastro-Enteritis, Addenbrookes Hospital, Cambridge; Dr Richard Petty at the Allergy Clinic, London, and Francesca Topolski, ASK registered kinesiologist at Neal's Yard Therapy Rooms, London. I am also indebted to the talented team at Boxtree, Rosemary Sandberg and Claire Bowles Publicity for their unfailing enthusiasm and support.

Introduction

Allergies are nothing new and have probably been around for as long as the human race. Reactions can be triggered by almost anything, from dust, mould and pet hair to bacteria, chemicals, and of course, food. The food we eat, along with an increasingly polluted environment, is increasingly responsible for causing allergic reactions – and the number of sufferers is growing: conservative estimates put it at 30 percent of the population.

Allergies change with eating habits. For example, now that soya is used widely in food processing – in the form of soya milk, soya protein, texturised soya, soya flour, etc. – many more people are becoming sensitive to it. Eating needs to be taken seriously if you want to keep your health. It's no good relying on take-aways and convenience foods, or monotonous, repetitive diets, and then complaining about allergies and digestive problems. A healthy diet needs to be honed from fresh, natural foods that have had little or nothing taken away.

Detecting and diagnosing a common food allergy may be difficult. In this *Quick Guide* you will find all you need to know about the different techniques available, as well as details on how to carry out your own exclusion diet safely. If you, or any member of your family, suffer from food allergy problems, I sincerely hope this *Quick Guide* will be an aid to a healthier future.

Liz Earle

—1—

All About Allergy

Do you have any of these symptoms?

* Headaches and migraines
* Abdominal bloating or cramps
* Frequent diarrhoea and/or constipation
* Eczema or other skin problems
* Painful swelling of joints
* Unexplained mood swings
* Depression or anxiety
* Swollen hands, ankles, feet, eyes, face
* Unexplained weight gain
* Catarrh, sinus congestion, runny nose
* Constant fatigue.

These are some of the most common symptoms related to food allergy. In fact, food allergy is thought by some to be at the root of many seemingly untreatable conditions and complaints – and the difference between feeling good and feeling lousy could be as simple as taking one or two foods out of your diet.

Allergy Facts

* Wheat and milk are two of the most common 'problem' foods
* There seems to be no rule as to which food causes which particular reaction – people react in different ways to the same food

* Allergies can affect almost any part of the body
* If you are allergic to one food, it is very likely that you will react to a number of others as well
* The foods eaten most often are the ones most likely to cause problems.

What Is an Allergy?

The whole subject of food allergies is highly controversial and much disputed, leaving most of us rather confused and certainly no clearer about what we can do about them. In the medical and health care professions views on allergy are wide ranging – some doctors and specialists do not accept that food allergies exist at all; while others feel that allergies are common and lie behind many diseases like eczema, arthritis, migraine and even autism.

In 1993 five people died from eating peanuts. Fatal allergic reactions like these tend to make headlines. However, thousands of people are thought to suffer from less severe reactions that are none the less undermining to their health. If you think you might have a problem with certain foods, then you have nothing to lose by finding out which foods they are, and taking steps to improve your overall health and quality of life.

The two things that seem to be the most disputed in the allergies field are:

* What the word actually means
* The various methods of allergy testing

Strictly speaking, an allergic reaction is caused by an oversensitivity of the body's defence system to a specific substance. In a true allergic picture, the immune system is always involved. In this type of reaction, the body regards a particular food or combination of foods as a poison. Every time that food is eaten, the immune system goes on alert, antibodies are produced and an adverse reaction is caused, which may range from an asthma attack to vomiting, or even death.

However, there is a growing body of medical evidence which demonstrates that allergens can react with other parts of the body as well as the immune system. These reactions are often referred to as intolerances or sensitivities. For example, it is now thought that food intolerance may play a part in some cases of autism. (A psychiatric disorder that occurs in approximately one in every two thousand children, with a prevalence in boys.) Symptoms of autism include head-banging and other self-mutilatory behaviour, and a craving for food and non-food items. Some parents report that autistic episodes are exacerbated when children eat certain foods such as chocolate, bananas, cheese and apples, and parents of autistic children themselves often have allergies.

There is no known cause for all cases of autism, but recent research carried out by Dr Waring at the University of Birmingham indicates that allergy or intolerance plays a part in some cases. Her studies showed that forty out of forty-two autistic children tested were unable to metabolise certain chemicals that have a toxic effect inside the body. These substances 'seep' into the central nervous system and can interfere with brain signals, leading to the altered behavioural patterns that are characteristic of autism. However, this research is still in its infancy and more studies are needed to establish the link between autism and food allergy.

Certain other factors can play a part in food intolerance, such as hypoglycaemia, PMT, stress, glandular imbalances, fatigue and digestive problems. For example, you may only react to a particular food if stress is a factor as well – during unstressful times that same food may not cause a reaction. You may only need to eat a tiny amount of the allergen, or a lot. You may need to eat it several times in succession to get a reaction, or you may get delayed reactions up to three days later.

True food allergies are easier to detect, as there is a reaction every time that food is eaten. Food intolerances are like shifting sands, in the sense that the body may or may not react every time, depending on what else is going on. Generally, allergic reactions are faster and more severe than food intolerances, and the reactions can be fatal. However, the symptoms are much the same for both and can affect almost any part of the body.

Most health practitioners apply a fairly loose meaning to the word 'allergy', encompassing the whole range of definitions including classic allergic reactions, intolerance, sensitivity, hypersensitivity and maladaptation. Whether allergic in the classic sense, or just hypersensitive, makes little difference to the sufferer. The main point is that, if you have an adverse reaction to a food which does not bother most people, then that's all that really matters.

This *Quick Guide* uses the wider meaning of the word 'allergy' in an effort to explain simply and clearly what sort of symptoms you might get and what steps you can take to eliminate them, and by doing so, improve your overall health.

Symptoms

A food that causes depression in one person may cause a skin rash in another and a runny nose in another. Some people suffer from several symptoms, some of which may be related to food, and others to something else, like chemicals or house dust mites. We are each unique, with a unique reaction to the foods that bother us. Some allergic reactions can be very subtle: a low-grade headache, a tight ring finger, a day or two of depression, a bout of anxiety or fear. Reactions can also masquerade as other problems, eg an allergy affecting the respiratory system can be seen as an infection in that area and not as an adverse response to a food. Other reactions can be most insidious, like weight gain and addictions.

Some of the most common symptoms include: a constantly runny nose, fluid retention, weight gain, headaches, skin complaints, arthritis, asthma, gastrointestinal complaints, menstrual disorders, hypoglycaemia and behavioural problems.

For many people, the idea that the foods they know and love are the very things causing their ill health is hard to accept. How can eggs bring on a migraine, cheese produce hallucinations, strawberries cause a rash, or bread lead to depression? Anyone who suffers from allergies knows that reactions can be severe, weakening, unwelcome, even fatal. However, the very fact that the most commonly eaten and best-loved foods are likely to be causing problems makes it all the harder to give them up.

Why Do We Get Allergies?

An intolerance to environmental substances and foods is a by-product of a changing world. It is a rule of evolution that creatures adapt to their environment over time and show better adaptation to the things they have been exposed to longest. In terms of food, we have been exposed longer to vegetables, fruit, meat, fish, seeds, nuts and berries than to grains and dairy products. Starches as a basis for nutrition are a relatively recent thing – thousands of years, as opposed to millions of years of eating things like roots and berries.

There are many theories as to why we seem to be suffering more from allergies now than at any other time in history. Many ecologists feel that the use of chemicals and oil products has grown far faster than our ability to adapt to them, and it is this which is causing people to suffer from allergies. As we continue to pollute our environment, we will continue to stress our defence systems. Our natural detoxification systems can only handle so much, and the more we stress our bodies the more likely we are to react to our environment, and that includes the foods we eat.

To put it simply, our bodies can only handle a certain amount of toxins before we get overloaded and become ill. In most cases, allergies are the body's way of crying for help. If we keep on loading ourselves up with toxins and other things that don't agree with us, we become more and more ill.

Other health experts believe that normally harmless foods shouldn't cause allergic reactions if certain health factors are taken into account. These include eating food in its natural state, free from chemical fertilisers and pesticides, additives and preservatives. Of the 7,000 individual food ingredients now in use, many are artificial colourings and chemical additives, which are commonly a constituent of the vast array of prepackaged and frozen foods that make up such a large part of our diet.

It is very common for allergies to go hand-in-hand with a vitamin and mineral imbalance. This can either be caused by inadequate diet or lifestyle factors. It can also happen indirectly as a result of a failure to absorb nutrients properly, as in the case of coeliac disease, or otherwise impaired digestion. It is most important to pay attention to your nutritional status and general health, as a lack of essential nutrients does seem to be an underlying cause of allergies. Certain vitamins and minerals are essential to the health of the immune system, and so, again, a lack of these may predispose us to allergy.

Some people react very badly to the gluten in cereals, especially wheat gluten. Because of this intolerance, the small intestine fails to function properly when there is any gluten in the diet, and this leads to a condition known as coeliac disease. Once this happens, patients cannot absorb nutrients properly and other problems thus arise.

To help avoid food allergies we also need to eat a wide variety of foods. Most allergies are caused by the foods we eat most often. How many of us get through a day without having wheat or dairy produce in the diet somewhere. Remember that both these foods are very widely used and appear in most processed foods in one form or another.

Here's an example of how easily refined starches, sugars and dairy products creep into a day's eating:

Breakfast	Plate of wheat cereal Milk and sugar 1 slice of toast, butter and marmalade 1 cup of tea with milk
Mid-morning	1 cup of coffee with milk Currant bun
Lunch	Cheese and salad sandwich Packet of crisps and an apple 1 cup of tea with milk
Supper	Pasta dish with green salad Apple pie with custard 1 cup of tea with milk

Did you spot seven starches, five sugars and eight loads of dairy products? The above diet is by no means an exaggeration and many people who eat like this might find health is improved by eliminating wheat and milk for a while (see Chapters 3 and 4).

Other problems contribute to the allergic picture, such as impaired digestion, poorly working bowels, enzyme deficiency, liver damage, candida infection, stress or hormone imbalance. Eunice Rose, founder member of the National Society for

Research into Allergy, believes that almost anything, from tap water to carrots, can cause an adverse reaction in someone whose digestive system is ill-equipped to deal with it.

What it comes down to is that the air we breathe, the water we drink and the food we eat is a direct link to the environment. It is vital that what we take in is of good quality, but we have witnessed lately a great abuse of both our food and our environment. Is it surprising that diseases affecting our immune system are on the increase? We can't keep adding chemicals and pollutants to the environment, consume large amounts of denatured and nutrient-poor foods and expect to stay healthy.

WHY SOME PEOPLE AND NOT OTHERS?

There are many factors involved in whether someone will develop allergies or not.

Inherited Predisposition

There is evidence that allergies tend to run in families and, although the same symptoms may not be present in other family members, there will be a general susceptibility. Which organs and systems in the body are strong or weak is another important factor and can determine how the allergic response will manifest itself. For example, someone with an inherently weak digestive system may suffer from bloating and discomfort after eating a 'trigger' food, or suffer from bouts of diarrhoea. If there is a respiratory weakness, then asthma might be the allergic response.

Bottle-fed or Breast-fed

Whether a baby is breast-fed or bottle-fed also plays an important role. Bottle-fed babies are more likely to develop allergies because they don't get a 'preview' of the diet to come, or the benefits of their mother's own immunity, which is passed on through her breast milk. Breast-fed babies are less likely to develop allergies either in infancy or adulthood (see Chapter 5).

Correct Weaning

Weaning is most important in setting the scene for future health. A baby's digestive system is imperfect and food needs to be introduced at the right pace for its development and tolerance. Weaning onto 'difficult' foods, like grains, too early can also cause allergic reactions (see Chapter 5).

Diet

The quality of the diet is hugely important, as is variety. A good-quality, natural, varied diet helps to prevent both food and chemical allergies, whereas a narrow and unhealthy diet tends to encourage problems.

The above are just general indications and may help to explain why you or your child have allergies. However, a breast-fed child may still be allergic, and a bottle-fed baby not.

HOW WIDESPREAD ARE ALLERGIES?

Estimates vary from less than 1 percent of the population of developed countries to as many as 80 percent, which just goes to show how tricky the subject is. Dr Richard MacKarness, author of an excellent book on allergies called *Not All in the Mind* (Pan, 1976) estimates that 30 percent of all people going to their GP have symptoms traceable exclusively to food or chemical allergy, 30 percent have symptoms partially traceable to allergies, while 40 percent have symptoms which are unrelated to allergies.

It might be surprising if we *weren't* allergic to the improvers, emulsifying compounds, artificial colourings and the host of potentially toxic substances added to food to make it look more tempting, give it a longer shelf-life and, therefore, increase its commercial value.

Different Types of Allergic Response

How people react depends on individual constitution, diet, lifestyle, etc. A string of symptoms could be caused by one food. Some people may get migraines or headaches; others can become violent. It may be easier to accept that foods like shellfish or strawberries can cause a spectacular swelling of the lips or a violent rash, but harder to accept that bread or milk is causing bouts of diarrhoea or depression. Daily exposure to common foods can cause and maintain chronic symptoms and many common ailments can be caused by a constitutional inability to metabolize starches and sugars properly. It wasn't until the 1920s that allergists began to suspect that day-in day-out exposure to commonly eaten foods might be what was causing chronic illness on a wide scale.

Some diseases that have been found to be associated with allergy include ME (myalgic encephalomyelitis), irritable bowel syndrome, arthritis, eczema, asthma, candidiasis (thrush), migraine, obesity and hypoglycaemia.

One of the problems with detecting which foods, if any, you are allergic to, is that allergies are often 'masked' or hidden, and reactions can be fixed or variable. If it is fixed, then you have a reaction every time you come into contact with that food. If it is variable, then, often, other factors need to be present simultaneously, for example stress, menstruation, hormonal changes, etc. In other cases, a combination of foods may cause problems, but not those same foods eaten separately – you may be able to eat peaches, and eat cream, but not peaches and cream together at the same meal!

There are three stages in the allergy process: alarm, adaptation and exhaustion.

ALARM

You get an adverse reaction pretty soon after exposure and the speed and strength of that reaction leaves you little doubt as to what caused it. For example, some people react extremely quickly to seafood, with an immediate swelling of the tongue on the merest contact with a prawn or piece of crab. Another typical reaction would be a baby being sick after drinking cow's milk.

ADAPTATION OR MASKED ALLERGY

The body learns to adapt to allergens. Although the trigger foods are still being eaten, the response is minor in comparison to the alarm stage. As part of the adaptation process, the adrenal glands help the body to cope by producing enough adrenalin and cortisone to keep the system stable. It is part of our evolutionary process that we change and adapt to new situations in order to survive, and so this adaptation to 'problem' foods is part of our survival mechanism. As long as the body's defence systems and hormones are in good working order, it can keep trying to adapt, but, over time, the adrenal glands gradually become exhausted.

During this phase, when you first eat a trigger food you feel immediately better and symptoms connected with an allergic response may be delayed for up to three days. Thus, the food causing the allergy goes unnoticed because the link between the food and the symptoms is hard to make. If the allergen is eaten regularly, then you don't feel the effect of the adverse response because you are constantly in the initial 'uplifted' stage. This explains why foods that are doing you the most harm are often the ones you desperately crave.

Not surprisingly, a common symptom of 'masked' allergy is a lack of energy, as the body is constantly trying to deal with the substances that are causing it problems. The concept of masked allergies is often hard to grasp, as you feel better if you eat the trigger and lousy if you don't, yet they are the very foods that can be at the root of chronic illness.

EXHAUSTION

The adaptation, or masked, phase places a huge stress on the body's defence system. The adrenal glands become shrivelled and exhausted and the immune system becomes damaged and so the third phase, that of exhaustion, is reached, in which the body hasn't the resources to fight any more. This phase is a bit like the alarm stage, in that you feel bad when you first eat the allergen, but the difference is that you also feel ill if you don't. As the adaptation fails, the pick-ups grow shorter and the hang-overs grow longer. The adrenal glands can no longer produce enough hormones to keep the system stable and so the hang-overs start to predominate and you feel under par most of the time. Many people seek help at this point and go to their doctor or health practitioner with common and constant symptoms such as total fatigue, bloated abdomen and depression.

The speed at which someone arrives at this stage depends on many factors, such as constitution, powers of elimination, lifestyle and eating habits.

Allergy Threshold

The point at which someone will react to a certain food is not necessarily fixed – it can change from day to day or from week to week. If other things are an influencing factor, then they will determine whether you react or not. In this way anything that raises your general health, such as stress relief, positive outlook, fulfilling life, healthy diet, satisfying relationships, etc. will raise the threshold. Conversely the threshold can be lowered by stress, infection, poor nutrition and unhappiness.

Allergy and Addiction

People with addictions to various foods or drink are not just weak-willed creatures who can't say no. Food addiction is one of the strangest aspects of allergy and affects as many as half of allergy sufferers. Often, people are not aware of their addiction because they unwittingly choose foods with that addictive ingredient in it. For example, someone with a wheat addiction may start the day with a wheat-based cereal and toast, have a digestive biscuit mid-morning, a sandwich of some kind for lunch, and finish off the day with a plate of pasta, never giving much thought to the huge amount of wheat that they are eating – just in one day!

As with other addictions, like chocolate, cigarette smoking or alcohol, people are sometimes aware, but still find it impossible to give up, as every part of their being seems to crave that substance. It's a bit like being a heroine addict, and just as hard to give up. If you're unable to stop eating a particular food or drink for one whole day without cravings, then you can be pretty sure that you have an allergic addiction to it.

Allergic addiction is a feature of the masked allergy phase, where trigger foods give you temporary boost, or a 'high', and later you feel bad, crave that food again (which makes you feel better) and often plunge into bingeing. The only way to feel better is by continuing to eat that food which, of course, perpetuates the problem.

In terms of allergies, it is often the foods we eat most that give us problems. The worst offenders are grains and dairy products, which in Britain and other Western countries are usually eaten every day, if not several times a day. The idea that wheat and milk could be at the root of many health problems tends to cause disbelief, but more and more people are discovering this to be true. In most cases people are unaware that these common foods are causing them problems just because they are eating them every day and have forgotten what it is like to feel fully well. The other factor that tends to make people dismiss the fact that common foods could lie at the root of their health problems is that many of them are hailed as being healthy foods, if not essential to health. This leaves many people confused and uncertain as to how to proceed.

—— 2 ——
Symptoms and Allergy Testing

As mentioned in Chapter 1, symptoms of allergy are wide ranging and can affect almost any part of the body. This makes them difficult to detect, especially if they are masked or hidden. The following is a list of complaints that can sometimes be caused by allergies, but it is worth noting that many of these symptoms can also be caused by other diseases and you need to be sure that these have been ruled out. But, if your doctor cannot point to any other cause, then food allergy may be the answer and you have nothing to lose by finding out.

Symptoms Caused by Allergies

Abdominal pains
Alcoholism or cravings for foods, tobacco, drugs; bingeing; constant hunger; nausea
Asthma; breathing difficulty
Bloating or discomfort after food; bowel cramps; colic; wind; heartburn or indigestion
Bruising
Chest pains
Dizziness; violence, rage; melancholy
Epilepsy
Excessive sweating; night sweats; sudden 'chill' or 'hots'
Extra sensitivity to touch in some places

Fatigue or tiredness not helped by rest; lethargy; sleepiness after eating

Feelings of confusion; forgetfulness; periods of poor concentration; inability to think clearly

Flu-like symptoms

Fluid retention; puffy face, eyes, hands, legs, ankles; overweight or underweight, obesity

Frequent cystitis

Glue ear

Headaches and migraines

Hyperactivity or restlessness

Hyperactivity in children

Hypoglycaemia

Irritability; mood swings; depression; nervous tension, anxiety, fear

Irritable bowel syndrome; constipation; diarrhoea; anal itching

Itch – with or without a skin rash; blotches or hives (nettle rash); eczema

Learning difficulties

Loss of confidence; feelings of detachment or unreality, of being an 'onlooker'

Mild fever

Mouth ulcers; bad breath

Muscle weakness or general weakness

Numbness; tingling or burning sensation

Racing or fluttering pulse; palpitations

Rheumatism; aching muscles; stiff neck; arthritis; stiff or painful joints; backache; face ache or face tenderness

Ringing or whistling in the ears (tinnitus); repeated ear infections in children; fluctuating deafness

Sleep disturbance

Sneezing or itchy nose; runny nose; watery eyes; blocked or inflamed sinuses; mouth breathing or snoring

Swelling of the tongue, mouth, lips
Swollen or tender glands
Vaginal discharge; menstrual disorders

Quite a list isn't it? However, it does stress the point that symptoms of allergy can be wide ranging and affect almost any part of the body.

What Can You Do?

A good place to start is to write down the nature of your symptoms, their frequency and severity. Have you checked these things out with your doctor? If so, and no solution is apparent, then you can be more certain that allergy is the root. The next step is to identify which foods, if any, are causing problems.

In some ways, symptoms are only partly helpful in indicating what is causing reactions, as it is hard to pin a particular food to a particular reaction. At one time it was thought that the point where the symptoms occurred was the route of entry. This would mean that respiratory problems are caused by substances such as pollen, house dust and petrol fumes; digestive problems by foods; skin complaints by things you touch. Nowadays it is generally accepted that any food can cause almost any type of reaction in the body.

When you are beginning to identify the foods that might be causing certain symptoms, it is worth taking into account that some symptoms do have prime suspects and it is worth concentrating on these first.

Nasal and breathing problems are often caused by things you breathe in, like dust, house dust mites, pollens, moulds, animal hairs, feathers and chemicals. Eczema and digestive problems are often caused by food and so on, but remember to keep thinking laterally – they may also be caused by chemicals you inhale. Keep an open mind – mental and emotional problems are as likely to be caused by inhalants as foods, and many people find they feel depressed when they eat bread or other wheat foods.

Some people develop allergies in association with other diseases such as candidiasis (often called thrush), Crohn's disease, irritable bowel syndrome, hypoglycaemia, etc. and it is essential to get these areas of your health sorted out as well, either by your doctor or a well-qualified alternative health practitioner.

Trigger Factors

Sometimes a food will only cause a reaction if other factors are present at the same time. These are called trigger factors. For example, stress can set off an allergic reaction to a food that you can normally tolerate. The time of year could be a trigger. For example, a mould-sensitive person may only have allergic reactions to foods in the autumn months and be free of symptoms for the rest of the year, while a pollen-sensitive person may only have reactions in the summer.

EXAMPLES OF WHAT TO LOOK FOR

* Time of year; season
* Time of day – are symptoms worse in the morning or evening?
* Weekdays or weekends?
* Location – at home, at work, abroad, etc.
* After strenuous exercise
* Stress, emotional upset, anxiety
* Viral infection
* Low blood sugar

* Hormonal changes – menstruation, ovulation, etc.
* During pregnancy

There are numerous other trigger factors, but it gives you an idea of what to look out for. Ask yourself what else was happening at the time of the reaction. Many women find they only suffer reactions during menstruation; others only after childbirth. Overwork, anxiety, bereavement, money worries, depression, can all trigger reactions that wouldn't normally happen.

Some can link their symptoms to a certain event or period, like an accident or an illness, and often say they 'have never felt the same since ...'. This could be due to taking a course of antibiotics or other medical drugs, such as the contraceptive pill. An accident may have damaged their skeletal structure, placing unusual stress on the body.

Addiction

Another thing to remember, when detecting the foods that are giving you problems, is that the food causing your symptoms might be the one to which you are addicted. If there is any food that you think you couldn't do without for a few days, then suspect it first! Some people will be prepared to give up almost any food until you hit on their allergic addiction and suddenly they will do almost anything to keep that food in their diet. The foods most commonly eaten and those most loved are probably the ones causing the problems. Harsh, but true!

Most Common Food Allergens

* Wheat, corn, oats and rye
* Milk and other dairy produce – especially cow's milk

* Eggs
* Chicken, pork
* Soya
* Sugar
* Yeast
* Citrus fruit – oranges, lemons
* Potatoes, tomatoes, onions, garlic
* Tea, coffee, alcohol
* Chocolate
* Peanuts
* Shellfish
* 'E' numbers (food additives – colourants, flavourings and preservatives).

Apart from the foods themselves, you need to be aware of other things that can make certain foods a problem. Contaminants like pesticide residue or synthetic preservatives and additives can cause allergic reactions. Many people find they can eat a particular food if it is organic, but they can't tolerate the same foods from a non-organic source. When looking for the culprits, you need to take as many factors into account as you can.

Other Factors Worth Considering

FOOD ADDITIVES

It's estimated that over 3,000 chemicals are used in the food-processing business and many of these we know only as a number. Not all food additives are bad for you – some of them are vitamins and minerals – but it is highly likely that others are. Many of the colourings, eg tartrazine, have been linked with hyperactivity in children, monosodium glutamate with so-called 'Chinese Restaurant Syndrome', and other additives with asthma. It is all very well listing an E-number on food labels, but it still leaves most people none the wiser as to what the additive actually is.

What, for example is E100 or E102? If you have a hyperactive child, perhaps you should find out. E100 is curcumin which is a natural additive and thought to be safe, whereas E102 is tartrazine, which is synthetic, and often implicated in food allergies. You will find a handy additive decoder in the *Quick Guide to Baby and Toddler Foods*, which lists all the E-numbers with their descriptions. Generally, artificial additives are implicated in many allergic problems including skin complaints, hyperactivity, asthma, and excess mucus.

Additives can be split into broad groups – colourings, emulsifiers, stabilisers, thickeners, synthetic sweeteners, acids, bases, anti-caking agents, flavour enhancers, glazing agents, improving and bleaching agents. With this cocktail of extras, it is no wonder our bodies complain.

As consumers we have the right to question what we are eating. Will sausages containing nitrite and nitrate preservatives give us stomach cancer, allergies, or any other illness? One of the problems with an additive is that, eaten on its own, it may be safe, but a cocktail of additives may not be. You need only pick up a packet of dried soup to find a host of emulsifiers, flavourings, colourings and preservatives, so one has to wonder what effect this mixture could have.

It is difficult to prove that food additives are harmful. However, certain health problems have been documented among people who work with additives in the food industry and their complaints include dermatitis, asthma and bronchitis. The relationship between additives and hyperactivity is well documented in Maurice Hanssen's excellent reference book *E for Additives*. Some of the additives that are allowed in Britain are banned in other countries. For example, of sixteen artificial colours allowed here, all are banned by at least one other European country.

FOOD CONTAMINANTS

Our food is becoming increasingly contaminated by residues of chemical pesticides, herbicides and fertilisers. In some cases, crops are sprayed up to twenty times during the growing season and these chemicals end up in the food chain.

Some chemicals, like DDT, although banned in Britain and the US, are still widely used in other countries. How do we know which countries are using DDT on which crops shipped into UK supermarkets?

Our meat and poultry can also get contaminated by chemical residues in the animal feed, not to mention the widespread use of antibiotics to keep disease at bay and growth hormones to increase yields. Some allergic responses may be due to these factors alone and not to the food itself.

WATER

Yes, even water should come under the microscope when seeking to find the cause of your allergies. Tap water contains elements used in the treatment process, including aluminium salts, chlorine and fluoride. On top of this, traces of chemicals used on the land eventually end up in our rivers and streams. For example, Drs Jonathan Maberly and Honor Anthony relate, in their book *Allergy*, that a sample of water taken in Essex was shown to have 160 different chemicals in it. Often, people find their symptoms get better or go away altogether when they stop drinking tap water and change to bottled or spring water.

The Next Step

Now that you have an idea of what to look out for, you can begin to find out what food or foods are giving you reactions. Always remember that anything and everything that goes into your mouth is a possible culprit, and that includes licking the gum on envelopes and stamps!

You may already have an obvious suspect, so you can begin right away to eliminate it from your diet. There may be a trigger factor that you can identify, like being in a certain environment or when in contact with pets, and these need to be avoided as well. If it is something in your work environment like the ink from photocopy machines, or dust, then you may even need to consider moving jobs, or perhaps altering your working routine.

KEEPING A DIARY

One of the best ways to discover what you are allergic to is to keep a diary. Record everything you eat and drink and any symptoms, to see if a pattern emerges. Also, record what you have been doing and the places you have been to. Ask yourself questions such as:

* Do I feel ill after certain foods?
* Does this happen every time or just sometimes?
* How long do the symptoms last?

In this way, by recording everything that you eat or drink each day and noting all adverse reactions, you can begin to see if any pattern emerges. It might be that you only feel lousy after breakfast, or only at weekends. You may get immediate reactions like bloating or cramps after a meal, or not get symptoms for hours afterwards. Keeping a diary will help you see which foods you eat frequently, and which you rarely eat. It will also help you to chart your moods and physical symptoms with greater accuracy. Often, when we go to the doctor with a complaint, it is hard to remember exact details of the nature, frequency and severity of the complaint, and if food allergy is at the root then it is difficult to spot without exact details.

When writing down what foods you eat, be specific. For example, if you have a tin of soup, write down its flavour and the ingredients listed on the label.

A Food and Activities Diary

DAY, TIME, PLACE	FOOD	SYMPTOMS
Tuesday		
9.00am, Home	Muesli, cow's milk, tea with milk	Feeling bloated and a lack of energy
11.30am, Office	Coffee with milk, banana	Clear
1.15pm, Office	Cheese sandwich, cup of packet soup, 2 apples	Clear
2.30pm, Office	No food	Feeling tired and lethargic
4.30pm, Office	Cup of tea and milk, chocolate biscuit	Felt better
7.15pm, Home	1 glass of white wine	Felt better
8.15pm, Home	Wholemeal pasta and pesto sauce, green salad, tomatoes, olive oil and vinegar	Felt full up and a little bloated
10.15pm, Home	Cup of tea, digestive biscuit	Clear

The above is an example of a typical day, but remember to record everything that enters your mouth. This may include vitamins and minerals, cigarettes, peppermints, licking envelopes and stamps, tap water, etc. After a few weeks a pattern may begin to emerge which will show up as something like feelings of lethargy an hour after eating sweet things or feeling bloated after eating wheat. You may only feel unwell in the office and not at home. Anything you think of that will help you track down what foods or drinks are causing you problems is worth making a note of.

Keeping a food and symptoms diary may be enough on its own to help you to track down the culprit foods, but sometimes it isn't possible to solve an allergic illness without seeking qualified help. Cutting out culprit foods and avoiding trigger factors may not be enough if the illness is deep and complicated, in which case you should seek expert help, either from your doctor, an allergy clinic, or a professional in the alternative medicine field.

When keeping a food and symptoms diary, remember to record:

* Everything that passes your lips
* The time the food was eaten
* Relevant details like the brand of a prepared food and list of ingredients
* Record all symptoms, the time they happened, how long they lasted, and their intensity on a scale of 1 to 10.

Allergy Testing

Allergy testing is a practical way to discover which foods you are allergic to. However, none of the techniques available are 100 percent accurate; most are, at best, 60–70 percent accurate.

None the less, some method of pinpointing allergens is necessary and testing is a valuable part of the discovery process.

There are several different methods of allergy testing – some conventional, others most unconventional – which are carried out by doctors, clinics, laboratories and health practitioners. Which method you choose really depends on what appeals to you, what you can afford, and what is available in your area. Some of the more commonly used tests are listed below. The more information you can gather yourself about the nature and frequency of your symptoms, suspect foods etc., the more efficient the results will be.

ELIMINATION DIET

This is one of the most reliable ways of detecting food allergies. It involves taking one or more foods out of the diet for at least five days, and then reintroducing the eliminated foods, one at a time, into the diet to see if there is an adverse response. During the exclusion period, any substances which are affecting the system adversely will be eliminated from the body. If your symptoms improve or, better still, disappear during this time, then you can be fairly sure that a food allergy is causing your problems.

One of the best things about elimination diets is that they unmask hidden allergies. Usually, after five days, patients are free of offending foods and become hypersensitive, so that when trigger foods are eaten again there is a marked and definite reaction which leaves no doubt as to what caused it. As described in Chapter 1, the difficulty in detecting masked allergies is that you are not aware of the symptoms relating to any particular food because the offending food is usually the one that is eaten most frequently. This makes an elimination diet a wonderful tool in detecting hidden allergies.

For some people it will take longer than five days for foods to leave their system. Others can have delayed reactions of up to forty-eight hours, which makes the reintroduction of foods a lengthy process, and it could cause nutritional deficiencies. Anyone who does embark on an elimination diet needs to be aware of the commitment that such a rigorous regime demands and of the need to be thorough. On the other hand, you will feel an enormous sense of achievement when you discover an allergen.

RAST TEST

RAST stands for radio allergo-sorbent test and is a method of identifying specific blood antibodies to certain foods and other substances. It is a conventional test and only picks up true food allergies (ie those in which the immune system is involved) and so is limited in its ability to pick up intolerances or sensitivities. Like other testing methods, it has its supporters and detractors, but from the patient's point of view it is expensive and is limited in its diagnosis.

SKIN PRICK/SCRATCH TEST

This is a commonly used testing method that looks at how the skin reacts to a suspect substance. A small amount of a prepared food is placed on the arm and then a scratch is made in the skin at that spot. If the patient has a sensitivity to it the skin will flare up and produce what's known as a weal. The bigger the flare-up, the greater the sensitivity to that substance. Once the problem foods have been identified, the patient is given an injection of, initially low doses of trigger foods until they can tolerate quite strong amounts. This is called desensitisation. Many people do not rate the accuracy of this type of testing as being much more than 40 percent and treatment rarely produces a permanent cure.

CYTOTOXIC ALLERGY TEST

This test is carried out in a laboratory by skilled technicians and involves exposing live white blood cells to a range of foods.

Depending on whether the cells become damaged or not, and to what extent, the level of food sensitivity can be assessed. One of the problems with this type of testing is that the results can be difficult to interpret and mistakes are easy to make. There have also been recent stories in the press and on the radio about several samples from the same person being sent away for diagnosis and each sample coming back with a different list of foods to avoid! However, it is said to be 70–80 percent accurate in the hands of experienced technicians.

COCA PULSE TEST

This is one of the simplest testing methods and uses the patient's pulse rate to diagnose allergies and sensitivities. It was invented by Dr Arthur Coca, who discovered that pulse rate increases suddenly by ten or more beats per minute following ingestion of a culprit food. It is a simple test that is easy to do at home and can help you to identify for yourself possible allergens. It is more efficient if you first go on an elimination diet and then test the foods as they are reintroduced. However, it is worth bearing in mind that many other things can cause a sudden rise in pulse rate.

Some of the more unconventional and controversial testing methods are carried out by practitioners of alternative medicine and, although thought of as highly controversial by the orthodox medical profession, they can be pretty accurate in the hands of an expert.

MUSCLE TESTING/SYSTEMATIC KINESIOLOGY

This method of testing uses the body's own systems to help discover the true cause of ill health and to find the necessary treatment to relieve symptoms. It is based on the theory that specific muscles, when gently tested, can reveal a great deal of information about the body's state of health.

Using systematic kinesiology, the practitioner can detect various imbalances and stresses that are adversely affecting health. In terms of allergies, the tester may find that certain foods cause particular muscles to weaken, which thus indicates the problem food. Kinesiology can also be used to detect any underlying cause of the allergy, ie whether it is a physical problem, such as irritable bowel syndrome, *candida*, digestive problems, or an emotional or hormonal problem. Systematic kinesiology uses the body to ask it what it needs (and what it doesn't need) in order to be healthy. It is a quick and easy way of testing, about 70–80 percent accurate.

VEGA TESTING

This method measures the body's electromagnetic reaction to the various substances being tested. By using electrical probes, a complete circuit is made between the patient and the machine. A phial of food is then placed in the machine, within the circuit. The body's electromagnetic response to that food registers on a meter and this shows the tester whether the substance is stressing the patient and to what degree. The machine is first calibrated by putting a phial of poison in the circuit. This normally registers on the meter as a drop in the current and any subsequent food substance that also causes a drop in the current is suspect. Certainly, any food that causes as much of a drop as poison shouldn't be eaten! Like other methods, vega testing should be carried out by a qualified practitioner and is thought to be 60–80 percent accurate.

HAIR ANALYSIS

You may come across adverts for hair analysis in connection with allergy testing, but this is certainly not one of the most accurate methods. Hair analysis involves breaking down the protein element of the hair to determine its mineral content in order to detect if there are any deficiencies. A lack of certain minerals and vitamins *will* cause health problems, but as a method of diagnosing allergic response, it doesn't seem to be very efficient.

DOWSING

Dowsing is one of the most unconventional testing methods, but it does work for some people and is largely dependent on the skill and sensitivity of the dowser. Typically, the dowser uses a pendulum to diagnose allergic response. The patient holds a suspect food while the dowser swings the pendulum. If the swing alters, it indicates a problem with that food. This is a quick and inexpensive way to detect allergies and is reasonably reliable in the hands of an experienced dowser.

As you can see, there are several methods of testing available, ranging from the scientific approach to the seemingly inexplicable. All of them have a place in this field of medicine. If there was only one accurate method of testing for allergies, it would no doubt have become universal by now. Many of the more alternative methods are gaining increasing support while others are being fine-tuned. It is worth telephoning different practitioners to find out how they test, and talking to your doctor or an allergy clinic before you decide which method of testing and course of treatment to embark on.

Whatever the results, allergy testing is only part of the story, as allergic reactions are the body's way of crying out for help. The next step involves healing the body. Treatment needs to be holistic – while physical symptoms are addressed, other areas of your life need to be looked at too, such as stress levels, relationships, job satisfaction, lifestyle, exercise, posture, etc. Anything which helps to take the load off the whole being will be a step in the right direction towards relieving allergies.

Allergy and Toxicity

A toxified body is more prone to be allergic, as it is having to deal with too many things at once. If you eat potential allergens on top of an overloaded system, then it's not surprising that it complains. Treatment needs to include cleansing the system from the inside with a good detoxification programme, so that the body has a chance to heal. Many underlying problems, such as digestive failure and irritable bowel syndrome, will have a chance to recover when trigger foods and toxins are removed for a while. This will also give the immune system a chance to strengthen. Detoxification and correct nutrition (which may include mineral and vitamin supplements) are essential parts of dealing with allergies (see the *Quick Guides* to *Vitamins and Minerals* and *Detox*).

——— 3 ———
Common Food Allergens

Milk and Dairy Produce

Milk is among one of the commonest allergens, yet it is one of the hardest foods to exclude from the diet, as it has such widespread use. At one end of the milk debate, we are led to believe that it is the perfect food, providing a readily available source of calcium, protein and other valuable nutrients. At the other end, we are told it is difficult to digest, inhibits the absorption of nutrients and causes allergies.

Other foods can supply the diet with adequate calcium, including vegetables, beans, nuts and grains. Tinned sardines are a very rich source of calcium. To prove the point, there are many tribal communities in the world where no dairy produce is eaten at all, yet children grow up with healthy bones and teeth, and diseases such as osteoporosis and arthritis are unheard of.

WHY MILK MAY BE BAD

The main problem with milk is if the body is unable to properly digest the milk sugar, known as lactose. About two-thirds of the world's population cannot properly digest lactose, while the remaining third only have a partial ability.

We begin life with plenty of the lactose-digesting enzyme, lactase, which enables us to thrive on our mother's milk as a complete and perfect food, but we eventually lose this ability as we get older, and so, if milk continues to feature in the diet, it causes all sorts of digestive problems and leaves us wide open, not only to a milk intolerance, but to other intolerances as well.

Rather than being a perfect food, milk becomes difficult to digest, is acid and mucus-forming and upsets the proper environment of the intestinal system, which ultimately leads to malabsorption of vital nutrients. People with a milk intolerance often experience abdominal bloating, intermittent diarrhoea, eczema and digestive problems.

Dairy produce, in general, has the same negative features of milk, although goat's milk and sheep's milk seems to be better tolerated by some people. Out of all the diary products, live yoghurt is the best option, as it is low in saturated fat and is already partially digested by friendly bacteria. These bacteria help to keep the intestinal environment right.

AVOIDING MILK

You really have to be on your guard when looking for hidden sources of milk. Remember omelettes and batter. Also, suspect all sweets and desserts. Some sweeteners, food supplements and monosodium glutamate have lactose as a 'filler'. Other milk-based ingredients to watch out for are casein, caseinate, lactose, and whey.

During a period of eliminating milk from the diet, you may get withdrawal symptoms in the first few days. After several months of avoidance you may find that you can return to eating small quantities of milk or cheese, etc. without any adverse reactions. By taking problem foods out of the diet for long enough, the body gets a chance to heal. There may then come a time when you can eat those foods again in normal, but not excessive quantities. Remember that the foods most commonly indicated in allergies are those most frequently eaten, so don't go back to having dairy products more than once or twice a week.

ALTERNATIVES TO MILK

Goat or sheep's milk (if they can be tolerated)
Soya milk (choose calcium-enriched)

Nut creams can make good substitutes for cream (make by puréeing almonds or cashews with a little soya milk or water)

Non-milk margarines

Ghee – clarified butter (although check that you are using ghee made from vegetable oils, and remember that even non-dairy ghee is high in saturated fat)

Soya-based 'cheese' spreads

Soya desserts and yoghurts

Wheat

In Britain we eat more wheat than any other grain, making up roughly 25–30 percent of the average diet. It is generally thought to be a wholesome, fibre-rich food, supplying many of the B group of vitamins, vitamin C, iron and protein. Unfortunately, some people find that wheat is the cause of allergic symptoms including depression, wheezing, digestive problems, irritable bowel syndrome, constipation and arthritis. Apart from obvious sources such as bread, pasta and cakes, it finds its way into a host of processed and commercially prepared foods.

WHY WHEAT MAY BE BAD

The biggest problem with wheat is gluten – a sticky glue-like substance which can play havoc with our digestive system by slowing it down and inhibiting the absorption of nutrients. Try rolling a piece of bread between your palms – see what a sticky little ball it becomes and think about what your digestive system has to cope with every time you eat bread!

Gluten is wheat protein. It is difficult to digest and encourages the growth of unfriendly bacteria, like *candida albicans*, which are responsible for producing toxins in the bowel. Symptoms such as constipation, diarrhoea, bloating, indigestion, wind and irritable bowel syndrome often disappear when wheat is removed from the diet. Many people feel tired, irritable or depressed after eating wheat, but because it is such a ubiquitous food, they rarely relate their symptoms to it. If gluten is the problem, then you need to be aware that rye, oats and barley also have a relatively high gluten content. People with coeliac disease (hypersensitivity to gluten) should avoid all such grains.

Another negative point is that over 97 percent of cereal crops in Britain are sprayed with one or more pesticides, and residues of these could be at the root of your symptoms as much as the wheat itself.

AVOIDING WHEAT

As with dairy produce, you have to be a bit of a detective and read all food labels thoroughly. Wheat often masquerades under less well-known names, such as fillers, cereal binders, cereal fillers, cereal protein, starch, edible starch, modified starch or protein. In general, beware of anything containing flour, any bakery product (cakes, pastries, biscuits), all foods sold in powder form, sauces, pies, sausages, burgers, etc. and grain-based drinks, eg beer, whisky, gin.

ALTERNATIVES TO WHEAT

Buckwheat – flour, flakes, spaghetti and pasta shapes
Flour alternatives – chestnut, potato (farina), lentil, chickpea
    (gram), tapioca, yam, soya
Rye flour, bread, crispbread
Rice cakes, flour, flakes, puffed rice
Oats, oat cakes
Non-wheat pasta, rice noodles
Alternative thickeners – arrowroot, corn flour, kuzu
    (Japanese seaweed extract)
Wheat-free soy sauce
Rice bran, soya bran, oat bran
Wheat-free mixes for sausages, veggie-burgers, bread, cakes

Gluten-Free
There are plenty of gluten-free breads, cereals and biscuits available these days. Also, try rice cakes, manna bread, sprouted grain breads or loaves

Yeast

Many people can develop a yeast allergy (especially if they suffer from an overgrowth of *candida*) with symptoms such as: digestive problems, bloating, sugar cravings, alcohol cravings, fatigue, depression, moodiness, and the more obvious symptoms of cystitis and thrush.

AVOIDING YEAST
Watch out for: pure yeasts, yeast extract (Marmite), anything containing vinegar, all alcohol, ginger beer, stock cubes, antibiotics and vitamin B supplements. Yeast often masquerades as hydrolysed protein, hydrolysed vegetable protein and leavening. If you are yeast-sensitive then you may also be sensitive to other mould and fungi-containing foods, such as cheese, mushrooms, peanuts and malt.

ALTERNATIVES TO YEAST
It is very difficult to replace yeast with anything else. You can try soda bread, sourdough bread, chapatis, yeast-free rye bread, rye crispbread, yeast-free bouillon mix.

Eggs

Eggs are also a common cause of allergy and, like wheat and dairy produce, find their way into many processed and ready-prepared foods. Sometimes, what the hens were fed on is the trigger in eggs – for example, if the hens were fed grain coloured with carotene dyes to make the yolk more yellow, you may react to that and not the egg itself. If you react to eggs then remember that you may also react to chicken, and a reaction to either of these may be due to the feed, which includes corn and wheat.

AVOIDING EGGS

Once again watch out for cakes, pastries, biscuits, batter; also mayonnaise and other sauces, powdered products, mousse, egg pastas, ice cream, mince meat, wine and beer (finings). Again you have to think laterally and read labels thoroughly to detect hidden egg in foods. Eggs often appear in a list of ingredients under other names, such as albumen, ovalbumin, lecithin or emulsifier.

ALTERNATIVES TO EGGS

There are few egg replacements – look out for 'egg-free' products, though some may be so synthetic as to be hazardous in themselves. It is best to do without entirely.

Soya

Soya is becoming increasingly popular and is used widely in the food-processing industry. It is also another common food allergen. Over the last thirty years or so, soya has crept into everyday foodstuffs, mainly in the form of soya oil (in tinned tuna fish, vegetable oils, margarines), soya flour (used extensively in bread making), soya beans, and texturised vegetable protein (meat substitutes).

AVOIDING SOYA

There are obvious sources, such as soya milk and soy sauce. Also, beware of tofu and bean curd, miso and TVP. Soya can often masquerade as vegetable protein and lecithin and, unless the ingredients are labelled on bakery products, you can't be absolutely sure that soya flour has not been used as well as wheat. For alternatives to soya flour, use rice flour, corn flour or buckwheat flour. Goat's milk is a good alternative to soya milk.

Corn

Like soya, the use of corn has grown over the past thirty years and it is also becoming a common food allergen.

AVOIDING CORN

Obviously, corn-on-the-cob and sweetcorn should be avoided! Remember that corn is also known as maize and that corn is *not* wheat. Thus, Cornflakes, popcorn, corn flour, etc., are not good. Watch out for cooking oil. Corn also masquerades as dextrimaltose, dextrin, dextrose, fructose, glucose, glucose syrup, glucose tablets, cereal starch, edible starch, modified starch, starch, vegetable oil, sweetening, syrup. It is often used in corned beef, some instant coffees, as a cereal base for beer and lager, and in the glue on envelopes and stamps. For alternatives to corn, look to wheat, rice, buckwheat, rye, barley, millet – and their derived products.

If this seems like an endless list of no-nos, and you are wondering what on earth you can eat, there are plenty of substitutes around these days (for a list of stockists, see Useful Addresses). The fact that so many alternatives are available is testimony to the increase in allergy sufferers. The other thing to remember is that excluding foods may not have to be permanent – just long enough for your body to heal. The time may come when you can tolerate small amounts of these foods again.

Always remember these rules:

* Eat a *varied* diet
* Eat pure, unadulterated foods
* Experiment with eating and cooking in different ways
* Organise menus and shopping trips in advance
* Cook your own food, make your own juices, bread, sauces, soups, etc.
* Stop relying on convenience and fast foods
* Don't eat any particular food too often
* Try to eat organic foods, if possible, to avoid chemicals and colourings, etc.

Whatever your symptoms, a balanced diet of healthy eating and nutritional supplements, if necessary, will help strengthen your immune system, which will reduce your sensitivity to foods. A healthy diet can also help to heal underlying conditions such as candidiasis, hypoglycaemia and irritable bowel syndrome – often associated with allergies.

—4—

The Anti-Allergy Diet

Exclusion Diet

An exclusion diet involves excluding one or more foods from your diet in order to find out which are causing your symptoms. A period of exclusion gives your body a chance to tell you which foods are making it ill. How far you go with this type of diet really depends on how bad your symptoms are. Some people react to only one or two foods, while others can be allergic to as many as twenty foods.

Since a total exclusion diet is often unmanageable, especially for people with families and a busy lifestyle, a partial exclusion diet will often be enough to expose problem foods effectively without causing too much inconvenience. Exclusion diets should never be carried out on children unless under qualified supervision, as nutritional deficiencies can arise quite quickly, not to mention the trauma that a child may suffer by being denied certain foods.

It is also important that an exclusion diet is *total*. Whether you are excluding one food or several, even a tiny amount of the excluded food may prevent you from getting a clear result. You also need to be a detective in looking out for hidden sources of excluded foods.

All exclusion diets involve two processes: eliminating one or more foods completely from the diet for a given period of time; reintroducing foods one at a time to check for adverse reactions.

This method of testing has to be embraced with full enthusiasm and commitment, otherwise you won't get a clear result and all your effort and sacrifice will have been for naught.

SINGLE FOOD EXCLUSION DIET

If you have a good idea which food is causing you problems, then a single food exclusion diet may be enough. The culprit might be something like strawberries or prawns, or it may be a more commonly eaten food like milk or wheat. Although it may seem easy enough to exclude dairy produce or wheat from your diet, you really have to look for hidden sources of these foods if the period of exclusion is going to be effective.

Writing a food and symptoms diary for a few weeks prior to an exclusion diet will help you to pinpoint which are the culprit foods. Ask yourself these questions:

* Do I have an adverse reaction after eating a particular food?
* Am I addicted to any particular food?
* Is there any food I crave, or cannot do without?
* Is there any food I eat every day, or many times a day?
* Am I constantly feeling exhausted and run down?
* Am I constantly hungry?
* Can I never lose weight no matter how little I eat?
* Do I have erratic mood swings?
* Do my symptoms come and go?

You may decide to be professionally tested for allergies or do your own pulse test, but if you can't identify a likely suspect, then pick one of the most common trigger foods, eg wheat, milk, yeast, eggs, corn, coffee, tea, chocolate or oranges. There is no harm in eliminating a single food for a short time, but make sure that you make up for any lost vitamins or minerals by substituting other foods or taking vitamin and mineral supplements. For example, if you are cutting out dairy produce for a while and are worried about calcium intake, chick peas, tinned sardines and broccoli are all good sources of calcium.

If you decide to take nutritional supplements seek expert advice, as vitamins and minerals should not be taken in isolation. For example, taking one of the B group of vitamins on its own can unbalance the rest of the B vitamins, or by taking too much calcium you can upset the magnesium status, and so on. Any vitamin or mineral supplements taken during the exclusion period must be hypoallergenic (free of any substance likely to cause a reaction, ie gluten, wheat, lactose, sugar, colourings, preservatives or yeast).

Once you have decided which food to leave out, you can begin. To be effective you need to remove this food from your diet completely for a minimum of five days, preferably for two to three weeks, and no cheating! If you do cheat you will have to go back to the beginning of the exclusion period, or you just won't get a clear result. If symptoms subside or disappear, then you can be pretty sure that the excluded food is the culprit and there will be no need to embark on a more complicated exclusion diet. Many experts feel that, once a trigger food has been excluded for nine months to a year, it can be reintroduced into the diet without causing problems. However, you always need to be aware that if you return to eating that food frequently, then you may well begin to react badly again.

Withdrawal Symptoms

While on an exclusion diet you may find that you feel worse at the beginning – stick with it! Withdrawal symptoms are a clear signal that you have pinpointed the problem food, and as it clears your system you will begin to feel much better. After four or five days you should be significantly better. Symptoms of withdrawal include headaches, nausea, shaking, excessive sweating, irritability and fatigue.

Anyone with allergic addictions will almost certainly have withdrawal symptoms and find themselves craving that food. This short period will pass and you will be free from the health-damaging effects of addiction. Keep a picture in your mind of how well you are *going* to feel, to help you ride out the storm.

Challenging

To be absolutely sure that you have identified the culprit food, the next step is to challenge it. Before the challenge, write down how you are feeling, then eat the chosen food on its own – you may need just a little, or you may need a lot of it to get a result – and keep a note of any changes. If your reactions in the past have been severe and immediate, then a tiny amount of the suspect food will be enough to challenge, but if symptoms were not strong, then you may need to eat a lot of that food to get a reaction.

Most people find that their symptoms reappear within a few hours, but delayed reactions can occur hours or even days later. If you don't have a reaction, then eat some more of the suspect food to be absolutely sure. If further proof is required, wait a few more days and then challenge that food again.

Use the pulse test to check what is going on with your body. Take your resting pulse before eating the food, and then take it again several times over the following two hours. A rise of ten or more beats is a pretty reliable sign that the food does not agree with you. Use the pulse test in conjunction with symptoms to get the clearest results.

If you get unpleasant reactions during the challenge phase, you can alleviate them by taking Epsom salts, or drinking a pint of water with a teaspoon of sodium bicarbonate added. Don't continue challenging new foods until you are feeling better again.

It may be that you can include the food in your diet again as long as you eat it sparingly and infrequently. On the other hand, you may have to exclude that food totally from your diet.

The drawbacks of a single food exclusion diet are that it only identifies one food at a time – it may well be the case that two or three foods are causing problems; and, if it is a broad-based food like wheat, yeast, or dairy produce, you need to be extremely alert to hidden sources of these foods in order to exclude them completely. Even a tiny amount of that food can cause a reaction and give confusing results, so make sure you know exactly what you are eating during the exclusion period.

LOW ALLERGEN EXCLUSION DIET

This is a half-way house between single food exclusion and a total, or near-total, exclusion diet. It avoids the most common trigger foods while, at the same time, it allows you to eat a relatively normal diet. This type of diet also excludes processed foods which usually contain additives, flavourings and colourings. For the diet to be most effective it is best to eat organically grown foods, which reduces the likelihood of ingesting chemical residue and a host of other agricultural additives.

Foods You can Eat

Lamb and lamb offal
Game – rabbit, pheasant, venison
Fresh fish – no shellfish
All vegetables
Vegetable juice
All fruits – except citrus
Fruit juice – no citrus
Dried fruit – unsulphured
Potatoes, sweet potatoes, yams
Seeds – sunflower, pumpkin, sesame
Vegetable oils, sesame, nut oils – no peanut or corn oil
Grains – brown rice, buckwheat, millet, quinoa
Beans and pulses – kidney beans, lentils, chickpeas, butter beans
Sprouts – alfalfa, mung beans
Honey and molasses
Nuts – except peanuts

Salt and black pepper
Herbs
Spices
Herb teas
Bottled or filter water

Foods to Avoid

Eggs

Milk (cow's, goat's and sheep's) and all dairy products –
butter, cheese, cream, yoghurt, fromage frais, skimmed
milk powder.

Wheat, oats, rye, corn, barley and all their products, eg cakes,
pasta, biscuits, pies, flour

Citrus fruit – oranges, satsumas, lemons, etc.

Sugar, syrup, jam, chutney, jelly, etc.

Artificial sweeteners

Coffee, tea, alcohol

Chocolate

Vinegar and pickled foods

Yeast and yeast extract – Marmite, yeast pastes

Fermented products – soy sauce

Additives, colourings, flavourings, if not natural

Margarine

Salty snacks – crisps, Twiglets, etc.

Tinned foods

Stock cubes, packet soups, veggieburger mixes, etc.

Smoked, salted, cured foods

Any foods which you know give you an allergic reaction

Fizzy drinks, carbonated drinks, squashes, etc.

Coffee substitutes

Organising the Diet

For many people, the diet will take away the bulk of their
'normal' foods and leave them wondering what they can eat! If

you live on breakfast cereals, sandwiches and pasta dishes, then it will be a big change to cut these things out all at once. So be prepared before starting the diet – make sure you have plenty of the allowed foods in the house and plan ahead what sort of meals you are going to make. This avoids being caught short, getting too hungry and grabbing a quick snack of forbidden foods.

How Long on the Diet?
Generally it is best to follow the diet for a minimum of five days and preferably for two to three weeks. If your symptoms have disappeared after only a few days, you can begin reintroducing and challenging the 'forbidden' foods one at a time to see which are the triggers.

As with the single exclusion diet, as you reintroduce a food make a note of how you are feeling before and after, and if possible do a pulse test to double-check the results. Keep noting down how you are feeling. If a reintroduced food doesn't cause any reactions, it can then join the 'foods you can eat' list. Any food that does cause a reaction needs to be kept out of the diet. To get the best results, reintroduce foods slowly – no faster than one food per meal, and, if possible, at the rate of one food per day. In a few weeks you will have made a list of safe and unsafe foods.

LAMB AND PEARS DIET
This allows two foods to be left in the diet, plus bottled or filtered water. Lamb and pears might seem like an odd combination, but the reason why they are chosen is because they are rarely indicated in allergies and so are relatively safe foods for most people. A variation of this allows you to eat turkey and peaches, or rabbit and raspberries. If you are a vegetarian, try one of the other diets!

The principle of the diet is that you eat only these two foods for five to seven days and then begin reintroducing other foods one at a time. Because this diet is so restricted, it gives a chance for the system to clear, and unmask hidden allergies which are causing symptoms. Like the other exclusion diets, write down how you are feeling before you begin introducing new foods and keep a note of any adverse reactions. Keep a list of foods which cause no reactions and foods which do. The pulse test is most useful as a way of double-checking trigger foods when you are challenging.

Warning

A two-food diet is most restrictive and should never be done without professional supervision. Severe exclusion diets can compromise your nutrition, and it is advisable to seek professional advice about vitamin and mineral supplements during the exclusion period. The following categories of patients should not undertake this diet:

* Pregnant women
* Children
* Diabetics
* Epileptics
* Anyone with emotional disturbances
* Anyone with a serious illness.

TOTAL EXCLUSION DIET

This excludes all food for five days and is effectively a five-day fast. Drink only bottled spring water or filtered water and if you smoke, then stop! The idea is to completely clear your system of allergens. If you have a tendency to constipation, then take some herbal laxatives, Epsom salts, or even an enema to get your system cleared out.

The advantages of the total exclusion diet (and the two-food diet) are the following:

* It is the most effective way of unmasking hidden allergies

* Followed correctly, the results are more accurate than any other testing method
* It is the only way for highly sensitive people to build up a tolerable diet.

The main drawbacks of both diets are:

* Their time consuming nature
* They are difficult to combine with normal life
* Withdrawal symptoms
* Tiredness
* It can take a long time to build up a nutritionally sound diet again.

Once you have completed the five to seven days' fast, challenge foods one at a time, along with taking pulse tests, and begin to build up a nutritionally balanced diet again. Begin with foods that are least likely to cause problems – eat exotic or rare foods, like kiwi fruit, artichokes, rabbit, etc. If you find that several important foods are triggering reactions you must seek professional advice as to how you can design a nutritionally sound diet in the light of your allergies. People with multiple food allergies often find that a rotation diet helps in this respect.

THE STONE AGE DIET

The stone age diet is based on the foods that our hunter-gatherer ancestors would have eaten before they became farmers. Many people feel that the dietary habits adopted by developed countries over the last century are largely responsible for many of the chronic diseases that have become common-place in Western society, such as coronary heart disease, diabetes, high blood pressure, and cancer of the colon. Such diseases are virtually unheard of among the few hunter-gatherer populations still remaining in the world.

Even over the last forty years, our food has changed radically. Our diets used to be made up of fairly simple fare with few added ingredients, but now more and more food mixtures have come into common use and some ingredients (like wheat and milk) are included in a multitude of different products, which means they get eaten every day and often at every meal.

The stone age diet is a low allergen diet and is nutritionally balanced. Many people find great relief when they follow this way of eating. It is also simple to follow.

Foods You can Eat

All fruit – except citrus
Fresh fruit juices – except citrus
All game and fish
Free-range eggs
All vegetables
Fresh vegetable juices
All fresh nuts – except peanuts
Herb teas – avoid blends
Salt, black pepper, herbs
Filtered or bottled spring water

Foods to Avoid

Milk in all forms – except human milk
All milk products
All cereals and their products
Sugar in any form
Meat from domesticated animals – pigs, cows, sheep, etc.
Chicken
Eggs, unless free-range
Citrus fruit
Alcohol
Coffee, tea and related drinks
All manufactured foods – canned, packaged, bottled, etc.

All processed meat or fish – smoked, pickled, salted, etc.
Chocolate and cocoa products
Tap water
Spices
Drugs, tobacco, potions, remedies

There are some exceptions to the above list. A modification of the stone age diet includes live low-fat yoghurt, in moderation. The grains which are best tolerated by allergy sufferers are rice and millet and these too can be included, in moderation. Although alcohol is not allowed, sometimes it is hard to avoid, for example at weddings or celebrations, and so a little dry white wine or real ale is acceptable.

The stone age diet is similar to the low allergen diet and should be followed in the same way.

MEDICATION

Anyone who is taking medical drugs must consult their doctor before coming off them during the elimination period. Sometimes it is all right to discontinue a drug for a while; for others it can be dangerous, so always seek medical advice first.

TIPS FOR SUCCESS

* Reintroduce foods which are *least* likely to cause reactions *first* – this means you can quickly build up a base of safe foods and re-establish a balanced diet
* Once your diet is established and the trigger food eradicated, try not to eat any particular food too often. Any food that is eaten too frequently may eventually cause problems
* After a period of nine to twelve months, you can try to reintroduce former trigger foods. Eat them sparingly so as not to set off an allergy again

* Keep a detailed food and symptoms diary before and during the exclusion period and for a few weeks afterwards so that you can keep a watchful eye on reactions

* Seek professional advice if undertaking an extreme exclusion diet to make sure that you are eating a balanced diet

* Seek expert advice about vitamin and mineral supplements while on an exclusion diet

* Simplify your foods. Buy food in its natural state (organic if possible). Canned or bottled foods usually contain other ingredients such as sugar, salt, additives, etc. Frozen foods may also contain these

* A good diet is based on foods which have nothing, or as little as possible, taken away, which means no processed or refined foods. Every mouthful of food we eat should contribute nutritionally to our diet and the presence of additives is a pretty good indication that it is junk food

* Think about what you are buying. For example, salmon reared on fish farms may contain red colouring. Smoked fish are likely to be coloured yellow with tartrazine or sunset yellow. Smoked mackerel may have sugar and salt added. Dried fruit often contains sulphur dioxide – look for dried fruit that hasn't been sulphated

* After an exclusion period, don't return to old habits of eating a few things too often. Variety is the key to staying well

* If you do not see a major improvement after the exclusion period, then it may be that foods are not at the root of your problems. You may just need professional guidance to help you identify what is causing your symptoms.

CUTTING OUT TRIGGER FOODS

If you have a severe and immediate reaction to a food every time you eat it, then you may never be able to go back to eating that food. On average, nine months of *total abstinence* will be needed before you can tolerate that food again – but only if eaten sparingly! If you have been sensitive to a food in the past, it is likely that you will never be able to eat it in the same quantities as you did before. During the nine month exclusion, don't cheat, or it will take even longer before you can tolerate forbidden foods again. As a rule of thumb, for every time you cheat, you need to add another three days of abstinence. If a food is reintroduced too early, then either old or new symptoms may appear and a lot of hard work and effort will have been wasted.

If there are underlying health problems which are causing food sensitivity, such as candidiasis, bad digestion, bowel problems, hypoglycaemia (see Further Reading), then it is wise to get these things sorted out too, otherwise you will not have dealt with the underlying cause of the allergy.

Rotation Diet

Rotation diets are extremely useful in cutting down the allergic load, while at the same time allowing you to eat a balanced diet. They work best for people who can eat trigger foods occasionally without adverse reactions, but are not able to eat those same foods frequently. Some people develop new allergies very quickly and trying to eliminate trigger foods becomes like plugging a sieve. All it takes is a too frequent exposure to a food and new symptoms arise. Rotating foods helps to avoid the frequent eating of any particular food. Another principle behind the rotation diet is that, if you are allergic to a food, it is likely that you are also allergic to another food in the same family – for example, if potatoes cause problems, then tomatoes, peppers, or tobacco may do so too; if oranges are a problem, then possibly lemons are too.

The guidelines for a rotation diet are that no single food is eaten more than once in every four days, and no food from the same family is eaten more than once in every two days. To be absolutely safe, try not to eat an allowed food more than once on the allotted day, ie if it is a wheat day then don't have wheat for breakfast, lunch and supper! Despite the fact that rotation diets are a bit complicated at first and hard to sustain, you can have fun with them. The different combinations of foods will force you to experiment with new recipes and new ways of eating which, in the long run, will really benefit your health and well-being.

Rotation diets help to identify allergens, prevent the development of new allergies and help the body to cure itself by lessening the load.

EXAMPLE ROTATION DIET
Day 1
Pick foods only from the list below. Try not to repeat items or concentrate on one group.

    (a) Chicken, turkey, duck, goose, eggs, pork, ham

    (b) Celery, carrot, parsnip

    (c) Banana, orange, date, tangerine, grapefruit, lemon, lime, lychee, pineapple, papaya, mango

    (d) Maple syrup

    (e) Parsley, dill, fennel, turmeric, ginger, ginseng

    (f) Coconut, cashew, pistachio, Brazil

    (g) Tea.

Day 2
Pick foods only from the list below.

    (a) Lamb, mutton, venison, crab, lobster, prawn, shrimp, mussel

  (b) *Spinach, cucumber, courgette, pumpkin, squash, gherkin,
      beetroot, beet sugar*
  (c) *Feta cheese, goat's milk*
  (d) *Apple, melon, pear, currant, plum, cherry, gooseberry,
      passion fruit, peach, apricot, nectarine, strawberry,
      raspberry, blackberry*
  (e) *Rose hip tea*
  (f) *Hazel nut, almond, carob, liquorice*
  (g) *Pea, chickpea, lentils, beans.*

Day 3
Pick foods only from the list below.
  (a) *Lettuce, chive, asparagus, leek, artichoke, endive, chicory,
      onion, garlic*
  (b) *Olives*
  (c) *Avocado, tomato, aubergine, pawpaw, peppers, rhubarb*
  (d) *Sunflower oil, safflower oil, olive oil*
  (e) *Buckwheat, yam, potato, sweet potato*
  (f) *Sunflower seeds, pecans, walnuts, sesame seeds*
  (g) *Chilli powder, paprika, cayenne, cinnamon, spearmint,
      rosemary, sage, thyme, marjoram, oregano*
  (h) *Mint tea, chamomile, dandelion.*

Day 4
Pick foods only from the list below.
  (a) *Beef, veal*
  (b) *Cabbage, broccoli, Brussels sprouts, watercress, Chinese
      leaves, turnip, radish, swede, mushrooms*
  (c) *Cow's milk cheese, cow's milk*
  (d) *Grapes, raisins, figs, guava, kiwi fruit*
  (e) *Corn oil*
  (f) *Cane sugar, wheat, oats, rye, barley (malt), corn, rice,
      yeast, hops, chestnut*
  (g) *Pine nuts*

(h) Chocolate
(i) Mustard, bay leaf, clove
(j) Coffee.

This type of diet does take time, effort and planning, but brings relief to many allergy sufferers as they are not continually bombarded with trigger foods. For example, this type of diet makes it impossible to eat wheat every day and you may find that eating wheat every four days is fine and therefore you don't have to permanently exclude it. On the other hand, you might find that you have adverse reactions every fourth day, and so can be sure that one or more of the foods eaten on that day are the triggers. Rotation diets work well if followed exactly, so it is vital to keep a diary of what you are eating and how you are feeling while on the diet.

Like anything new, it will take time to get used to this way of eating and planning meals, but after a few weeks you will be in the swing of it as you begin to repeat recipes and get a grip of which foods are in which food families.

Rotation diets can be backed up by minerals and vitamin supplements, provided they are hypoallergenic. See Useful Addresses for stockists of hypoallergenic supplements.

Food Families

The following list will help you to put meals together. It gives many common foods and their families, but it is by no means all-inclusive. You will find some food products mixed in with the list of natural relatives, to aid identification.

PLANTS
Fungi or Moulds
Baker's yeast (includes breads, doughs, etc.), brewer's yeast

(includes alcohol), mushrooms, blue cheese, vinegar (including pickles and salad dressings, etc.)

Grasses
Wheat, corn, barley, oats, millet, cane sugar, bamboo shoots, rice, rye. (Buckwheat is not a member of the grass family)

Lily
Onion, garlic, asparagus, chives, leek, shallot.

Mustard
Broccoli, cabbage, cauliflower, Brussels sprouts, horseradish, radish, swede, turnip, watercress, mustard and cress.

Rose
Apple, pear, quince, almond, apricot, cherry, peach, plum, sloe, blackberry, loganberry, raspberry, strawberry.

Pulses or Legumes
Pea, chickpea, soya bean (includes soya milk and texturised soya), lentils, liquorice, peanut, kidney bean, string bean, haricot bean, mung bean, alfalfa, green pea.

Citrus
Orange, lemon, grapefruit, tangerine, clementine, ugli, satsuma, lime.

Cashew
Cashew nut, mango, pistachio.

Grape
Wine, champagne, brandy, sherry, raisin, currant, sultana, cream of tartar.

Parsley
Carrot, parsley, dill, fennel, celery, celeriac, parsnip, aniseed, caraway, coriander, angelica.

Nightshade
Potato, tomato, tobacco, aubergine, pepper, chilli pepper, paprika.

Gourd
Honeydew melon, watermelon, cucumber, squash, cantaloupe, gherkin, courgette, pumpkin.

Daisy
Lettuce, chicory, sunflower, safflower, burdock, dandelion, camomile, artichoke, pyrethrum.

Mint
Mint, peppermint, basil, marjoram, oregano, sage, rosemary, thyme.

Palm
Coconut, date, sago.

Walnut
Walnut, pecan.

Goosefoot
Spinach, chard, sugar beet, beetroot.

Sterculia
Chocolate, cocoa, cola nut.

The following commonly eaten plant foods have no commonly eaten relatives: juniper, pineapple, yam, banana, vanilla, black pepper, hazelnut, chestnut, avocado, fig, maple syrup, lychee, kiwi fruit, tea, coffee, papaya, Brazil nut, ginseng, olive, sweet potato, sesame (includes tahini).

ANIMALS
Ruminants
Cattle (beef, veal), milk and dairy products, mutton, lamb, goat.

Poultry
Chicken, eggs, pheasant, quail (not turkey).

Duck
Duck, goose.

Swine
Pork, bacon, lard (dripping), ham, sausage, pork scratchings.

Flatfish
Dab, flounder, halibut, turbot, sole, plaice.

Salmon
Salmon, trout.

Mackerel
Tuna, bonito, tunny, mackerel, skipjack.

Codfish
Haddock, cod, ling, coley, hake.

Herring
Pilchard, sardine, herring, rollmop.

Molluscs
Snail, abalone, squid, clam, mussel, oyster, scallop.

Crustaceans
Lobster, prawn, shrimp, crab, crayfish.

The following commonly eaten animals and fish have no commonly eaten relatives: anchovy, sturgeon (caviar), white-fish, turkey, rabbit, deer (venison).

For a more complete picture of food families, it is worth referring to *The Allergy Handbook* by Dr Keith Mumby.

Related Food

Apart from being related biologically, food is also related chemically. For example, a chemical like caffeine may cause all sorts of adverse symptoms and be a component of several foods that you unwittingly consume regularly. The chemical element which triggers your symptoms may not be in the same food family.

CAFFEINE
Caffeine is a stimulant and affects even a non-sensitive person, giving rise to insomnia, heightened alertness and palpitations. You will find caffeine in tea, coffee, cocoa, chocolate, some pain-killers, some cold and 'flu remedies, migraine drugs and some soft fizzy drinks. If caffeine is the problem, then all of these things will cause adverse symptoms, but if tea is a trigger and not coffee, then you can be fairly sure that it is not the caffeine which is the problem.

NICOTINE
Nicotine is found in tomatoes, potatoes and tobacco, which all belong to the nightshade family, but it is also found in cheese, chocolate and bananas, which are not related botanically. If you

have a nicotine sensitivity then you need to avoid these nicotine-containing foods or rotate them every four days.

GLUTEN

Gluten is the protein element of grains and is found especially in wheat, rye, oats and barley. People with coeliac disease cannot tolerate gluten and need to avoid all gluten-containing foods. Gluten-free produce is becoming readily available around the country so that grains can still be enjoyed without the adverse symptoms.

HISTAMINE

Histamine is a natural substance found in the body, but is present in only small amounts. An excess of histamine has been found to cause migraines and foods that have been kept for a long time, like tinned fish, cheese and salami, all have a lot of histamine. Other foods thought to be histamine-releasers are egg white, shellfish, strawberries, tomatoes, chocolate, fish, pork, pineapple, pawpaw and alcohol. You will need to experiment with these foods to find out if histamine is indeed the problem.

TYRAMINE

Tyramine has been found to cause migraines and rashes and can be found in cheese, tinned fish, yeast extracts like Marmite and Bovril, red wine, beer, cheese, avocado pears, oranges, bananas, eggs, spinach and tomatoes. If several of these foods are eaten at the same meal, it obviously increases the total tyramine load.

SALICYLATE

This has been found to cause allergic reactions like skin rashes, hayfever and asthma, and there is much controversy as to whether it is a cause of hyperactivity in children. Salicylate is found in aspirin, so anyone who is allergic to aspirin may also be allergic to salicylate in foods. Most fruits contain salicylate, especially dried fruit, and some vegetables (broccoli, cucumber, endive, radishes and courgettes). Also corn and some spices and herbs contain a lot (curry, paprika, thyme and rosemary). Synthetic salicylate is used as a flavouring and can be found in sweets, ice-cream and soft drinks. A high salicylate intake has been indicated in behavioural problems in children.

This is by no means an exhaustive list of chemically related foods, but shows that searching for allergies is not always a simple process and that you need to be aware of the many probable triggers.

Preparing for Exclusion or Rotation Diets

Preparation is the key to success and will really help you to sustain the exclusion period. Try to follow these guidelines before you set out on your journey of discovery:

* Have a chat with your doctor or health practitioner about what you are intending to do. You may want to be under their guidance or have a professional allergy test done. If you are on medication, check whether it is safe to come off it for a while
* Keep a food and symptoms diary to pinpoint the connection between certain foods and symptoms
* Make a list of current symptoms before the exclusion period. It is easy to forget how bad you once felt when symptoms are relieved
* Stop smoking. Come off the contraceptive pill and sort out an alternative. Give up alcohol
* Plan a good time to start the exclusion diet – ie a quiet period, either socially or at work

✱ Plan what you are going to eat and get rid of all forbidden foods. If you have allergic addiction you don't want temptation sitting in the fridge. If you live with other people, ask them to help you by keeping forbidden foods out of your sight and smell. Perhaps you have a friend or family member who can do an exclusion diet with you to give mutual support.

Once you are at a stage where you feel better and symptoms are relieved or have disappeared, you can move to a two-day rotation. This is closer to a normal diet, while still keeping to the principles of rotation. If any symptoms recur, then move to the four-day rotation for a while.

Vegetarian/Vegan

Vegetarians and vegans will have no doubt noticed how difficult and nutritionally compromising some of these self-help diets are. Some of the common allergens – milk, eggs, cheese, nuts, soya beans, yeast, wheat, grains etc. – are the staple foods of a vegetarian regime. In fact, part of the reason why many vegetarians have allergies is because they eat a lot of potential trouble-makers, while at the same time using menus which lack variety.

If you suffer from allergies, you may have to renounce your vegetarian/vegan principles for a short time, while you sort out your problem. After all, it is a small price to pay for the health benefits that will be reaped. If you just can't face that, then rotate your food as much as you can, while maintaining a nutritionally balanced and *varied* diet.

Case Histories

The following three case histories are recounted by a naturo-pathic practitioner, who has helped many people deal with their food intolerances and allergies.

Twenty-three-year-old female with severe PMT and constipation

This particular lady had always been constipated, even as a child, and she generally went for three to four weeks without a single bowel movement. When she did eventually have a bowel movement it coincided with the onset of her period. She also suffered from premenstrual tension (PMT) for ten days, experiencing black and tearful moods and generally wanting to withdraw from all company.

After taking all the relevant details into consideration, particularly her eating habits, it became apparent that wheat might be causing her constipation. The constipation was itself the cause of her PMT, as food was trapped inside her body and had become toxic, creating a chemical imbalance which affected her moods.

Within two weeks of adopting a wheat-free diet of natural, unprocessed foods, her constipation had cleared and she was even having a daily bowel movement! As a result, the symptoms of PMT were dramatically reduced and she felt much better.

Thirty-six-year-old female with depression and exhaustion

This lady had a two-year-old boy and complained that she had no energy to deal with him. She also sometimes experienced terrible black moods which made her want to throw her child out of the window. Now, this may seem like fairly normal behaviour to those who know how much hard work is involved in looking after a two-year-old.

However, a simple change in diet changed this woman's moods and energy levels dramatically. After a nutritional consultation, yeast was strongly indicated as a problem food, and the lady was put on a very strict yeast and sugar-free diet with no refined foods.

Three weeks later, she had renewed energy and the black moods had disappeared entirely. She has continued on this diet for nine months and says that she has never felt better and is able to enjoy being with her son in a way that she found difficult before. Occasionally, she can eat yeast, but if the old symptoms return she simply goes back to the yeast-free diet for a few weeks. So, in the case of this lady, an intolerance to yeast was the problem, not an allergy, as small amounts of yeast in her diet did not affect her.

Forty-year-old male with eczema

The patient complained of eczema, which he had suffered from all his life. There were short remissions from the skin condition, but he generally had eczema most of the time. Since dairy produce is often linked with eczema, this was eliminated from his diet, along with the other major allergens: wheat, corn, eggs, tea, coffee, yeast, alcohol and chicken.

Eczema is notoriously hard to control, but, after four months on this diet, the patient's eczema had greatly improved and rarely caused him to suffer as he had done previously.

—— 5 ——

Babies, Children and Allergies

Allergic problems frequently start in infancy with colic, eczema or asthma, often coinciding with bottle feeding, or weaning. Other symptoms include tonsillitis, earaches, runny nose, skin problems, bed-wetting, wheeziness, learning difficulties and hyperactivity.

Prevention Is the Best Cure

There is much you can do to prevent your child from developing allergies, especially before and during pregnancy and in the first two years of their life. This is a time when you can have almost full control over what your child eats and can establish their health for the future.

Remember that a proneness to developing allergies often runs in families, so if one or both parents suffer from allergies, the likelihood of the child developing them is high. Other factors, such as whether a baby is bottle- or breast-fed, plays an important role too, as does careful weaning onto a nutritionally balanced diet. A little effort on your behalf can go a long way to minimising the chances of your child becoming sensitive to food and help his or her resilience for the future.

In babies and children, food is a very common cause of allergic reactions, but you need to remember that other things may also be affecting your child, such as pet hairs, pollen, washing powder, etc. Keep an open mind when detecting what is troubling your child.

Pregnancy

Babies can be sensitised to foods even before they are born, because tiny molecules of food from the mother can reach the womb. This is why it is so important for pregnant woman to watch their own diet and be aware of the most common sources of food allergens.

If you are planning to become pregnant and suffer from allergies, then you can begin by seeking out which foods are causing you problems and cutting these out of your diet. Have a chat with your doctor or health practitioner for advice and dietary supervision, or you may wish to get in touch with one of the support charities, like Foresight, which offer practical advice to would-be parents.

Pregnancy is a time when you need optimum nutrition, both for you and your baby, and therefore it is most important that you seek professional advice before embarking on any type of elimination diet. You may also need nutritional supplements, and these should be correctly prescribed. If you have any underlying health problems, such as thrush, or low blood sugar, deal with these too. The healthier you are, the better the start your baby will have.

Breast or Bottle?

In terms of allergies, breast feeding and late weaning are great preventatives. A breast-fed baby gets the benefit of the mother's immunity, which is passed on through her milk, as well as a 'preview' of the diet to come. Breast milk contains antibodies that protect the baby against invading viruses and bacteria.

Breast milk also contains a substance called colostrum, which appears in the first few days of feeding, and which helps the baby's gut to function properly. If you find breast-feeding difficult for any reason, then at least feed for the first few days and you will have helped set up a healthier situation than if you went straight onto bottle-feeding. Breast-feeding is not a guarantee against allergies, but it is an important protective measure.

Although a baby may be breast-fed, if the mother is drinking cow's milk, some of this may get through to the infant through her milk and cause digestive problems. A sensitive baby can react to indirectly fed problem foods.

Weaning

Babies have underdeveloped digestive systems, which are more open to molecules of food leaking into the bloodstream and causing allergic reactions. As they grow older, so their digestive system matures, and they can more easily cope with different foods. This is why weaning too early can cause havoc with a baby's digestive system and leave it open to all sorts of sensitivities in the future. Careful weaning, like breast-feeding, can really help to give a child a good start in the battle against food allergies.

HELPFUL TIPS ON WEANING

* Wait as long as you can before weaning your child – if possible at least six months
* Introduce new foods slowly – one per day
* Introduce foods on their own, such as plain puréed carrots or plain mashed banana. Don't be in a rush to combine foods

* Keep a food and symptoms diary so that you can keep a check on any foods that might be causing allergic reactions
* If the baby shows no signs of reacting to a food, try it again after five days just to make sure that it hasn't been sensitised on the first eating. If there are still no reactions, add that food to their diet
* Keep your child's diet varied. No food should be eaten every day – they could build up a sensitivity to it.

FIRST FOODS

Avocado
Banana
Buckwheat
Carrots
Parsnip
Plain baby rice
Potatoes, sweet potatoes
Sago
Swede, turnip
Tapioca (only for totally breast-fed babies, as bottle-fed
*   babies will be getting tapioca through their formula feeds)*

SECOND FOODS

Fruit (except citrus)
Other vegetables (except cabbage family)

NOT BEFORE NINE MONTHS

Millet
Oats
Rye
Wheat

Not before twelve months

Beans, pulses, peas
Cabbage family
Citrus fruits
Corn
Cow's, sheep's, goat's milk and their products
Eggs
Fish
Meat
Nuts, seeds
Poultry
Sugar
Tapioca (for part or fully bottle-fed babies)
Yeast

This is a difficult regime to stick to, but can be worth it for a baby in a family with a history of chronic allergy symptoms. Most babies will thrive on this kind of diet, especially if they are still having the occasional breast-feed, along with any necessary vitamin and mineral supplements. The older your child is when first introduced to potentially troublesome foods, the less likely they are to develop a sensitivity to them.

Your doctor or health practitioner will be able to advise you about liquid forms of vitamins and minerals that are designed for babies and small children. If you are at all worried about your child's health and diet, always seek the advice of your doctor or health specialist.

Signs and Symptoms of Allergy

Whatever the symptoms, always consult your doctor first, if your baby is unwell, in case allergy is not the cause. However, these are some common symptoms to look out for:

* Constipation
* Diarrhoea
* Restlessness, sleeping difficulty
* Constant crying
* Irritable, unmanageable behaviour
* Hyperactivity
* Colic
* Eczema, dermatitis
* Vomiting, stomach aches

The best way to detect whether food allergy is at the root of the problem is to keep a food and symptoms diary for both you and your child. Breast-fed babies can react to foods that the mother is eating and this will help you to pinpoint what these might be, but remember that your baby may react to different foods. If you are not sure which foods to omit from your diet, then some of the commonest triggers are cow's milk (and its products), wheat, eggs, yeast and corn. Try leaving one or more of these out of your diet for five days and see if symptoms improve.

If your baby has had nothing but breast milk, then the probable culprits are foods that the mother is eating, or ones she craved or ate a lot of during the pregnancy. If the baby has had 'top ups' with bottled milk or has been fed exclusively on bottled milk, then suspect that.

If you are bottle-feeding with a cow's milk formula and think that is what is causing reactions, then you might try switching to a different type of feed. You could try a soya-based formula instead, such as Wysoy, nutrilon Soya, or Ostersoy. Remember that soya milk can also cause allergic reactions in some babies.

Other types of formulated baby foods include comminuted chicken formulas and hydrolysed formulas. Although the hydrolysed varieties are made up of cow's milk (and other foods) they are treated with digestive enzymes, which make them much easier for the baby to digest and a great deal less allergenic.

Look out for other triggers as well, such as bedding, vaccinations, viral infections, a new pet. Food may not be the only source of the problem. If your baby is only having bottled or breast milk, is he/she also having juice, medicine, toothpaste, or chewing on something that could be causing problems? Everything that passes his/her lips is a potential source of allergy.

Food-sensitive Children

Generally, symptoms are much the same as in adults, but some specifics include:

* Bed wetting
* Vomiting
* Tummy ache
* Persistent diarrhoea, constipation
* Glue ear
* Asthma
* Eczema
* Hyperactivity
* Sudden character change
* Headaches
* Fits
* Black rings under the eyes (known as allergic shiners).

ELIMINATING TRIGGER FOODS

First, you need to discover what is causing the symptoms – this may be food, chemicals, pollen, house dust, etc. You may want to get them professionally tested (see Chapter 2) or keep a food and symptoms diary as outlined in Chapter 4. After a few weeks you may be able to see a clear relationship between your child's symptoms and what he/she is eating. Some symptoms, such as recurrent sore throats or runny noses, may not be caused by allergies, but they may well be sustained by them. Once the trigger foods are removed from the diet, these may improve.

Never remove any nutritionally important food or food groups from a baby or child's diet for any length of time without seeking expert advice first. Children can easily become deficient in essential nutrients unless a careful watch is kept on their diet.

It is much harder to eliminate foods from a child's diet, as it is harder for children to understand why they can't have their favourite foods. Try to explain as best you can why you are not letting them eat a particular food or foods. If you explain, for example, that eating bread makes them have a sore tummy, they might be more willing to give it up. Perhaps the whole family could avoid the forbidden food as well, to support the child. You could also try introducing alternatives to the missing foods to make the diet as normal as possible.

If your child is at school age, then it is a good idea to have a chat with their teacher about what you are doing so that you can enlist their support. They may be able to take a lunch box to school with food that they can eat. Try to make their diet as normal and as flexible as you can.

Food Additives and Behaviour

Behavioural problems in children are a very common symptom of allergy and the relationship between hyperactivity and food additives has been well documented in recent years.

The main symptom of hyperactivity is the 'Jekyll and Hyde' phenomenon. One minute you have a little angel and the next, a little monster. Hyperactive children can be very disruptive to everyone around them and anyone who has experience of this will confirm how wearing it can be. This switching of personality for no apparent reason is one of the most obvious signs of a hyperactive child. Most children are naughty and disruptive at some time or another; hyperactivity is something other than just naughty behaviour.

According to the finding of a Canadian study, food allergy is indicated in 20 percent of cases of hyperactivity. It is now becoming recognised by the medical profession that a host of childhood problems, from eczema to behavioural problems, are caused by certain foods and food additives. The Hyperactive Children's Support Group has found that hyperactive children tend to respond very well to an additive-free diet. Two of the main offenders are tartrazine (E102) and sunset yellow (E110) which can be found in thousands of common foods, from sweets and fizzy drinks to sausages and peas. According to the the group, 59 percent of children suffering from hyperactivity are sensitive to monosodium glutamate (E612).

It's not surprising that, as the use of food additives has increased, so has the number of children suffering from hyperactivity. The notion that food additives could be at the root of behavioural problems in children was first proposed by an American doctor, Ben Feingold. He also claimed that food not containing additives could have the same adverse affect.

When searching for reasons for why your child is behaving badly, always consider other things that may be going on in his life, too – food or food additives may not be the complete answer. Are there other problems, such as difficulty at school, sibling rivalry, home insecurity, etc.? If it is purely a case of allergy, then, most likely, physical symptoms will be present as well as behavioural problems, such as stomach aches, rashes, diarrhoea, constipation, etc.

Symptoms of hyperactivity

* Irritability, grizzliness
* Overactive, constantly on the move
* Short attention span
* Explosive moods, wilfulness, disobedience
* Clumsiness, accident prone
* Insomniac, wakes constantly
* Demanding, moody
* Uncooperative, disruptive
* Learning difficulties, poor concentration
* Aggression, destructiveness.

If you think your child has one or more of these symptoms, then have a chat with your doctor to make sure that something other than allergy is not causing it. If you feel that food or food additives are at the root of the problem, then you can start writing a food and symptom diary, or have your child tested for allergies. Food additives like tartrazine often cause an immediate response and so are fairly easy to identify. A drink of orange squash may cause your child to misbehave instantly. On the other hand, foods that the child eats every day, like wheat or milk, may not be so easy to spot, since reactions may be chronic and hidden. There may be nothing to indicate that these foods are causing him to lose control.

The Hyperactive Children's Support Group offers advice on elimination diets based on the Feingold diet. You may want to construct your own elimination diet based on the various options in Chapter 4. However, always remember that children are susceptible to nutritional deficiencies and any form of elimination diet should always be professionally supervised.

It is well worth sorting out a child's allergies early in life, since evidence shows that children with food sensitivities are more likely to develop problems when they are older.

Case History

Liz Earle – my story

Before writing this Quick Guide *I had experienced first hand what it is like to have a food intolerance or allergy in the family. I myself have had a problem with yeast for many years. If I eat yeasted bread my stomach bloats, my joints become puffy and I gain a few pounds. My limbs also ache and feel heavy and I get very lethargic. They say you are often intolerant of the foods you like the most and, for me, it is true. My favourite 'comfort' snack used to be a piece of toast or a crumpet. Nowadays I eat honey on rice-cakes! I also make sure my vitamin supplements are yeast-free.*

My children also have a tendency to food allergies. My daughter Lily reacts to the common food triggers tartrazine and sunset yellow. If she goes to a tea party and has a handful of Smarties I can tell the minute I collect her. Her normally sunny personality changes; she becomes difficult, hard to control – almost hyperactive – moody and has a glazed look in her eyes. She also sleeps fitfully in the night and grinds her teeth. If she has these food dyes several days in a row, it will make her skin itchy and trigger eczema. Fortunately, we have identified the problem and it is not serious as we don't have artificially coloured food in the house. I ask her not to eat brightly coloured things at parties, but it's not easy for a four-year-old!

My two-year-old son Guy has a mild milk intolerance. I first noticed this when I weaned him from breast milk onto cow's milk at around nine months old. He became very sneezy and had a persistently green, gungey nose. At first I thought this was a cold, but it spread and developed into an ear and chest infection. This was cleared with homoeopathic remedies and I decided to check his diet for trigger factors. He made an amazingly rapid improvement when he stopped drinking cow's milk. I used to have to change the sheet in his cot every morning as it would be covered with green gunge from his nose.

Now he never even gets a sniffle. Guy is fine with yoghurt and fromage frais, possibly because it is fermented, and I make sure he eats these every day to ensure he gets enough calcium for his growing bones. He has unsweetened, calcium-enriched soya milk on his cereal every morning and extra chewable calcium supplements to top him up. I hope he will eventually grow out of his milk intolerance. Every few months I try him with a small glass of cow's milk to test his reaction, but to date he has always responded with a snotty nose.

Jamie, aged twelve

Jamie's mother realised that her son had a milk intolerance even as a baby. He would cough and vomit after a feed and he suffered from constant diarrhoea. Jamie was brought up on soya milk and dairy substitutes, like soya margarine and cheese. Today, Jamie still has a mild intolerance to milk and yoghurt. If he drinks a glass of milk it makes him cough and his stomach bloat. Funnily enough, cheese is not such a problem, although it does affect him to an extent. Jamie avoids dairy products and is a fit, healthy boy with a passion for football and other sports.

Glossary

Acute – in relation to disease, meaning short term.

Allergen – a substance that causes an unnecessary immune response. The body sees the allergen as a potential or real threat and therefore reacts to protect itself.

Allergy – the condition of having a reaction to a certain substance.

Calibrate – to mark the scale on a measuring instrument.

Candida – *Candida albicans* is an unfriendly intestinal bacteria which, if it gets out of hand, can cause a range of health problems, such as allergies, mood swings, depression, cystitis, thrush, fatigue and digestive problems. Candida also weakens the immune system.

Candidiasis – the condition of having an overgrowth of the *candida albicans* bacteria. This can puncture the gut wall and leave people open to allergies.

Challenge – the process of exposing a person to an allergen, eg a food or any other substance to which they are intolerant, and observing the reaction. The challenge can be by eating the substance, touching it, or inhaling it.

Chronic – in relation to disease, meaning long term.

Cystitis – an infection of the urinary tract caused by an overgrowth of the *Candida albicans* bacteria.

Eczema – a red itchy rash on the skin which tends to flake and ooze, or weep.

Enzyme – enzymes are made of protein molecules and are the catalysts that aid chemical reactions in the body. For example, digestion requires digestive enzymes to properly break down food.

Gluten – the glue-like protein part of cereals such as wheat, rye and oats, responsible for many people's allergic reactions to these grains.

Hormones – hormones are secreted by the glands, eg adrenalin is secreted by the adrenal glands. They help to regulate bodily functions.

Hyperactivity – a behavioural disorder of children and sometimes adults, manifested by impulse activity, low stress intolerance, emotional instability, anger, anxiety, aggressiveness, destructive behaviour, slow learning and a short attention span. Hyperactivity is often caused by food additives, flavourings, colours and preservatives, pesticides, insecticides, fungicides, caffeine, tea, coffee, chocolate, refined foods, junk foods, food allergy, coeliac disease, heavy metal toxicity, vitamin and mineral deficiencies and hypoglycaemia.

Hypersensitive – excessive sensitivity to something. For example, many people are extremely sensitive to different elements in food, dust, flowers, drugs, etc. When they come into contact with the offending substance – whether by eating, inhaling or touching it, they develop certain characteristic reactions such as asthma, vomiting, diarrhoea, hay fever, eczema, etc. Such people are said to be 'allergic' to the offending substance.

Hypoglycaemia – low blood sugar. People with hypoglycaemia have difficulty keeping their blood sugar levels stable. Symptoms include nervousness, irritability, emotional problems, fatigue, depression, cravings for sweets, cold sweats, shakes, tiredness, allergies, anxiety, etc. These symptoms are usually improved by eating regular meals of whole, natural foods. Junk foods, refined foods, sugar and stimulants such as alcohol and caffeine all encourage hypoglycaemia as they rapidly increase blood glucose levels. The body is then stimulated to reduce these levels quickly, creating a state of low blood sugar.

Immune system – a complex army of cells and antibodies which protect the body from foreign invaders.

Intolerance – an inability to cope with a substance usually because of underlying health factors such as digestive failure, low blood sugar, etc. The reaction does not necessarily involve the immune system, and so is not an allergic reaction.

Irritable bowel syndrome – a disorder of the bowel characterised by chronic diarrhoea or constipation, or a mixture of the two.

Neutralisation – the use of individually-titrated, very low doses of an allergen to block the allergic reaction of the body to that allergen.

Syndrome – a collection of symptoms occurring together.

Toxin – poison.

Further Reading

GENERAL

Allergy? Susan Lewis. Wisebuy Publications, 1986.

Allergy and Intolerance: A Complete Guide to Environmental Medicine. George Lewith, Julian Kenyon and David Dowson. Green Print, 1992.

The Allergy Connection. Barbara Paterson. Thorsons, 1985.

The Allergy Handbook. Dr Keith Mumby. Thorsons, 1988.

The Allergy Survival Guide. Jane Houlton. Vermillion, 1993.

The Complete Guide to Food Allergy and Intolerance. Dr Jonathan Brostoff and Linda Gamlin. Bloomsbury, 1989.

Liz Earle's Quick Guide to Baby and Toddler Foods. Boxtree, 1994.

Liz Earle's Quick Guide to Detox. Boxtree, 1995.

Not All in the Mind. Dr Richard Mackarness. Pan, 1976.

Overcoming Food Allergies. Gwynne H Davies. Ashgrove Press, 1985.

SPECIFIC

All About Asthma and Allergy. Dr H Morrow Brown. The Crowood Press, 1990.

Candida Albicans: Could Yeast Be Your Problem? Leon Chaitow. Thorsons, 1985.

Cooking Without. Barbara Cousins. (Available from Moorside Natural Healing Clinic, 177 Moorside Road, Swinton, Manchester M27 3LD. This book claims to be suitable for candida, ME and allergy sufferers.)

Danger! Additives at Work. Melanie Miller. The London Food Commission.

Diet, Crime and Delinquency. Alexander Schauss. Parker House, 1981.

E for Additives. Maurice Hanssen. Thorsons, 1987.

Low Blood Sugar (Hypoglycaemia): The 20th Century Epidemic? Martin L Budd. Thorsons, 1981.

Stone Age Diet. Leon Chaitow. Optima, 1987.

Your Food Allergy Child: A Parent's Guide. Janet Meizel. Mills and Sanderson, 1988.

Useful Addresses

FURTHER INFORMATION AND SUPPORT

The British Allergy Foundation
St Bartholomew's Hospital
West Smithfield
London EC1A 7BE
Tel: 0171-600 6127
Helpline: 0171-600 6166
The foundation campaigns to increase public awareness of allergy and to advance knowledge and research.

The British Register of Complementary Medicine
ICM
PO Box 194
London SE16 1QZ
Tel: 0171-237 5165
They will supply a list of registered practitioners in your area.

Coeliac Society
PO Box 220
High Wycombe HP11 2HY
Tel: 01494 437278
Publish a regularly updated list of gluten-free products. Written enquiries only – send an SAE.

Food Commission
3rd Floor
5–11 Worship Street
London EC2A 2BH
Tel: 0171-628 7774
Consumer watchdog on food.

ME Association (Myalgic Encephalomyelitis)
Stanhope House
High Street
Stanford-le-Hope SS17 8EX
Tel: 01375 642466

National Association for Colitis and Crohn's Disease
98a London Road
St Albans AL1 1NX
Tel: 01727 44296

National Asthma Campaign
Providence House
Providence Place
London N1 0NT
Tel: 0171-226 2266
Helpline: 01345 010203

The National Eczema Society
Tavistock House East
Tavistock Square
London WC1H 9SR
Tel: 0171-388 4097

BABIES AND CHILDREN

Foresight
The Old Vicarage
Church Lane
Witley
Godalming GU8 5PN
Tel: 01483 427839
Offers practical advice to would-be parents.

The Hyperactive Children's Support Group
71 Whyke Lane
Chichester PO19 2LD
Tel: 01903 725182
Produce a range of information and literature to support parents as well as a handbook and regular journal.

National Childbirth Trust
Alexandra House
Oldham Terrace
Acton
London W3 6NH
Tel: 0181-992 8637
Provide information and have local support groups.

SUPPLIERS OF ORGANIC OR SPECIALIST FOOD

Henry Doubleday Research Association
Bocking
Braintree CV8 3LG
Tel: 01203 303517
Largest organisation of organic gardeners in the world. Products and gardening books available by mail order.

Green Farm Foodwatch
Burwash Common
East Sussex TN19 7LX
Tel: 01435 882482
Suppliers of specialist foods.

Foodwatch International Ltd
9 Corporation Street
Taunton TA1 4AJ
Tel: 01823 325022
Fax: 01823 325024
Technical advisory service and suppliers of specialist foods.

Natural Foods
Unit 14, The Sidings
Hainault Road
London E11 1HD
Tel: 0181-539 1034
Britain's largest home-delivery service for high quality organic produce including free-range and organic meat, fish and seafood and environmentally friendly household supplies.

The Nutri Centre
7 Park Crescent
London W1N 3HE
Tel: 0171-436 5122
Fax: 0171-436 5171
Suppliers of hypoallergenic nutritional supplements, specialist foods, a wide range of related books and cookbooks. They also have a mail-order service.

Real Meat Company
East Hill Farm
Heytesbury
Warminster BA12 0HR
Tel: 01985 40436

The Soil Association
86 Colston Street
Bristol BS1 5BB
Tel: 0117 9290661
They will supply a list of organic growers and farmers in your area.
This includes suppliers of organic meat and poultry.

ALLERGY TESTING AND TREATMENT

There are various avenues you can go down to get tested and treated for allergies. If you would like the conventional approach, then get in touch with your doctor and ask him/her for advice about what is available through the NHS. They may be able to refer you to one of the many allergy clinics for testing.

The Allergy Clinic
32 Weymouth Street
London W1N 3FA
Tel: 0171-352 6351

Cytotoxic Allergy Testing
York Laboratories
Tudor House
Lysander Close
Clifton Moor
York YO3 4XB
Tel: 01904 690640
They provide a cytotoxic allergy testing service as well as general
advice on allergy and nutrition.

If you prefer the alternative route, then there are several bodies which can refer you to a registered practitioner in your area.

British Complementary Medicine Association
St Charles Hospital
Exmoor Street
London W10 6DZ
Tel: 0181-964 1205

British Register of Naturopathy
328 Harrogate Road
Moortown
Leeds LS17 6PE
Send SAE for details of your nearest registered naturopath.

Council for Complementary and Alternative Medicine
179 Gloucester Place
London NW1 6DX
Tel: 0171-724 9103

Institute for Optimum Nutrition
13 Blades Court
Deodar Road
London SW15 2NN
Tel: 0181-877 9993

Institute of Complementary Medicine
PO Box 194
London SE16 1QZ
Tel: 0171-237 5165

Index